Ex Absurdo Sequitur Quodlibet

Moshumee Teena Dewoo
&
Nerisha Yanee Dewoo

Langaa Research & Publishing CIG
Mankon, Bamenda

Publisher:
Langaa RPCIG
Langaa Research & Publishing Common Initiative Group
P.O. Box 902 Mankon
Bamenda
North West Region
Cameroon
Langaagrp@gmail.com
www.langaa-rpcig.net

Distributed in and outside N. America by African Books Collective
orders@africanbookscollective.com
www.africanbookscollective.com

ISBN: 9956-792-35-7

DISCLAIMER
All views expressed in this publication are those of the author and do
not necessarily reflect the views of Langaa RPCIG.

And then one day
A bird sang blue

We were home

1. The poet of the sea

In waves of sadness
Are the melodies of time
The sensible intentions
The hyperboloid whispers
And the spineless pleonasms
That embrace the poet sane

In waves of sadness
Is an anchor, another god
Heavy, rusty
Drowned and concealed
That hungers for the poet opened
Conscious of his life a sacrifice

2. The darkest painting

I remember everything
I remember how you gave me what was left of you
Of me
In that room dishonest…
The cold, fiery breeze, faithful
Brushing your soft face
As the obsessive lover would,
Seeking the most vulnerable parts of you

I remember the melancholy of your body
The wisdom of your breath
And the stillness of your screams
You were the darkest painting
That I wished I had constructed
Layer after layer
The beauty of your soul exposed on my canvas
On days of painless torture

I remember how you counted the raindrops
Alone, languorously
Your reflection, undemanding, was indistinct in the misty
window

You listened to my heart beat that day

I remember that you were afraid that it would stop

Untouched, untamed

Fated

3. Gnosis challenged

You once said to me

That you believed love to be the religion of the spirit

The experience of infinity, inevitable,

Against the tyranny of selfishness

And antagonistic commitments

     I fell in love with your voice that day

     Again

4. When fear breaks through the rational self

I prayed today

For the first time

I prayed unsure of whom to implore,

What to ask,

How to

I prayed to a celestial creator

A benevolent listener

A myth

An apocryphal tale writ in countless tongues

I prayed interrogative of my need to do so

I held my head up high

To the obscenely grey sky

Hesitant

Suspicious of my lucidity

But I prayed

Slave to man

The language of evil beneath my feet

Ready to obey

In apotheosis

5. Mind and Matter

Braid a rope

From my vein

It will give me hope

I will not complain

6. A common state of mind

I am not missing

I am dead

A cemetery head

7. The space in between

Rare are the moments when the sound of the passing train
Does not take me away from my crowded mind

Rare are the moments when the train passes…

Damn
Damn
Damn the crowd
The noise
The fucking noise
Stop
Make it stop
Stop
The fucking noise in my head
In the world
The world
It does not hear the noise
It does not hear
What is in my head
Make it stop
Where is the train?
Where is this fucking train!!?

What a wreck!!

Train

Wrecked

On my neck

8. Propaganda against the unconscious

When I ran away
I left your voice behind
To find my own

9. I am not numb to you

Your silence pierces my soul
As your noise, my body

10. Revolution from within

Cry

The flow of your unwept tears

And the scars etched in your flesh and spirit

The pieces of your self

Pure

Scattered

Next to the fractures of your faultless wreckages

Scream, I beg you to

Leave

Surrender

Come back

Run to me

Run from me

No

Stop

I am terrified

So are you

Cry

Let me cry

Let me cry the flow of my unwept tears, my scars

Pieces of my person, scattered too

Next to the fractures of my wreckages

It is your turn again

To cry

Show me when you do

Cry so that I never forget about you

Cry

Play yourself on repeat

I need you to

I do not need you to

I do

11. A bond beyond blood

I have slept under foreign stars
For ten thousand nights already

       They are all that I have left
       You had to be the last to know

12. The silent observer

Beyond your spirit wind-torn

And your body wreathed

In piano strings

Is a light, Voyager

A light maiden blue

Blue jay

Finding it harder

And harder

To pen

The river sore

The tale drowned

And another

Dreams in a suitcase

The crown of lambs

Lions that crawl back to the circus

Twisted knives in outer space

The mother's hand that feels out of place

The child hiding under the table

The pale flesh of strangers

Fragile fires that last as long as a summer

Open doors to those whom we love

Birds that do not fly

Harmless ghosts that we meet on delicate stairs

Too many impalpable impressions

Exhausted pictures

Guarded guests at the table

Memories never returned

The hum of things never started

The broken recorder that was stolen

Perverted triumphs

And cracked sidewalks

That should not have spoken

13. Dead ends

The rhythmic inferno
Of a heart unattached to its body
Is the echo
Of all things unexplainable
And yet
Too easily achievable

14. Eternity

To the familiar eye
The soul divine
Devotion absolute
Is not unconsciable demand

      Only
      Devotion has a deadline

15. Bemused muse

Your skin

Emerald

Three eyes

Intoxicated

A God in your bed

You hunt

Furious Matangi

Your word, blunt

16. Textures

My cigarette burns

On the last traces of your self

That I absurdly kept

In between a summer

And a cold coffee

I take one last breath

One last glance

And the world stops

Agony

I lose control

My blood turns to ink

A short story turns into a chapter

A lullaby into raindrops

That fill the space

Between now and never

Between what is

And what could have been

I remember to blink

I love my lipstick

A stain

Transparent

That decorates my grief

Unkiss me

My cigarette burns

17. What I am and not

I could be as much of a fluke

As a divine entity

Whichever the case may be

I have not a clue

About how to make of me

A good story

18. The poison of life

More tragic

Than recognising

That I will one day

Lose the ones that I love

Is the realisation

That I do love

19. Powerlessness

Outside of me

Is everything

That I will never be able to set free

Inside

Is everything

That I cannot be

20. Marks on the soul

Would it truly be easier to let the experience, sad, drift from the rest of one's life story, until the memory thereof wanders, restlessly, mythical in the foggy thread of old illusions?

I wish for none to ever know

21. Fucking prey

The fleeting prey

Is eager

To flick

Fuck and

Play

Behind the smoke screens

Of where you stray

22. Of all things that bother me

The garret of your self will always be maddeningly

unknowable to me

23. I burn

I crave for your touch
Like the candle that never prays

      Constant
      Wretched

24. Reflect

How would I feel if I peered into a room that should have been empty and saw someone staring back at me?

25. Silence

Nods tell of half-anecdotes

And structured regrets

Buried deep

In dislocated reality

26. Grasp

The very thought of being surrounded by others
Is the smallest measurable unit of human connection
That can mitigate the symptoms of loneliness
Bringing relief to the aching chest
For a while, at least

27. Shadow

From her smile
You should have known
Her murmur sweet

28. Side kick

A man without wealth
Makes a mediocre felon
Who must climb walls
Bare his hands, weapon

29. A request

Please
Break me down

    I insist

30. Blueprints

I woke up

Obstinate

Inspired by a dream

To build somebody else

A person new

A person piercing

Unbent

Free

Freedom

Free

Demon

But I cannot move yet

A ladybug flew to my palm

She does not stir

She never did

Unwise

Bewildering

Poor little thing

She never stopped singing

Something about spells

31. Static

I overslept

Going beyond classical logic

       I do not want to turn around

32. Backstage

Was it ever worthwhile
For mighty men
To make kings of beasts?

33. Ghost

Your walls, Sugar
Like the beat of drums
Assumed sad jungle ballads
In the Congo
Mean nothing to me
They bore me
They are empty pages
Strings without marionettes
Just too many a rock
Stupid block
Knock, knock
Hello, Sugar
I am a passive aggressive crusader
I can help you
Knock
Knock your walls down
Into a private rave
Do not be afraid
The pill will help
I will shield you too
When it no longer can
I have my whole life ahead

No

More than that

Many more lives

Back where I come from, Sugar

I keep being born

Again

And again

And again

And again

34. Life senseless

Who broke the moon?

35. Otherness

For the most of us
What is originally planned as a short sojourn
Is, in the course of a few mistakes only,
Transformed into permanent disconnection
From that which we truly desire

36. The gap

I can tell you everything
But the colour of my soul

37. *La Presque-Fin*

I long for the day

When the mountains fade away

When the stars shine so close

And the rhyme, from my body

Finally goes

38. Mute

The music was loud. I wanted it to be

A woman waited to fall. Friends fought over her

A paper doll burned

I was trapped

Around, a thousand stones

As complex as my own

I sought comfort

You asked if I trusted you

I had no answer

You pulled me to you. I forgot about my feet sore

You worshipped the ruins. You kept the thought off my mind

I wished to feel your heart

I was too close. I was breaking the rules

We danced into ceremonious suicide

Out of rhythm

To our favourite song

We shared a beer

The bottle was green

As your eyes were

In the morning

Blackened that night

On bad boy dust, bright

39. Untitled

Skinny, skinny man

Man like no other

Whom, on a path barren

I met, briefly

You, yes, you

Skinny, lifeless man

I write about you

I must

I must tell the world

About the day that we met

You smiled at me

Do you remember?

It was a smile sincere

The kind that I had never seen before

Did I deserve it?

I smiled back

I wondered if I had touched you too

As you had me, with your skinny, gentle hand

On that path barren

I still wonder

Skinny, faceless man,

If you knew,

If you know

That since then, since you

I have grieved myself

To death

40. Drowsy eyes

The sun shines

Bright

Too bright

I ask for my sunglasses

I bite on a piece of old chocolate

Devotion screams next door

Will it ever stop?

Here, only unconditional love

A fine way

Our way

To trip

To truth

On wires unattached

What a fine way

To wear our masks

And sleep tight

Hands tied

Backed up

Under blankets of coal

Our doubts behind

What a fine way

Our way

To no longer belong

To no longer

Be

41. Bliss

If this is all you have
Then it is all I need

        Now shoot me to the ground

42. Power

All monsters cry

About how the bone breaks

How blood flows

How to make it stop

How to break a bone

How to make blood flow

At one

Two

Three

Four

Five

O'clock

In the morning

Before

And after

Being reminded that without the threat of pain

There would be no reason for us to live at all

43. Mr Never

I was finally promised
A little something to believe in

44. Uniforms

What would be of us
If we were not allowed
To parade the earth
Choked to the bone?

45. The sound of reality

I would break you
If I could glue you back together

    Yes
    It scares me
    Yes
    It should scare you too

46. Fact

When your breath finally slows
So will my heart

        This is not a promise
        I must make it clear

47. Syndrome

The machine King

Master of the controlled paradigm

Is, of the Queen of Stockholm,

Prisoner saccharine

    The only one

48. Inexperience

If she has not yet acknowledged the Sun

It is because of how petrified

She would be without

The thought, across, she has not yet come

49. Distinct

It is not about honouring those whom you love

      It is about honouring the love that you have for them

      Outside the consensus trance

50. In suspension

For a moment

Neither life nor death scares me…

Just for a moment

51. Lifelessness

Life is a tale built upon the vestiges of selfhood;

Yours

Mine

And everybody else's

52. Because I am the little lion man

Because she asked me to

I will raise her

To be worshipped

At the temple

Where lay the consequences

Of my schizophrenia

53. Shift

When I finally learned to walk
It was to the other side of the moon

It was then that I understood my nature asleep

54. Goodbye Royal

And then one day,

The world stopped spinning around you

55. The invisible

We have agreed
To a power show
A revelation
In motion slow that condemns
The lethal eye
Of the open mind

56. Where is the universe?

The raptured rational is perhaps the most believable reality.

Any other alleged form thereof is sheer cult - ego-utopic, ego-dystonic cult,

The hubris phase of a religious mania of inspiration,

A validated addiction to a one-dimensional, linear experience of the past, present and future

Symptomatic of a state of unfamiliarity with the true nature of being

57. Freedom

If I could

I would get rid of all the clocks

And dance to the melody of my core

Beyond my ego

But we do, we do

We do

Not need to

Talk about this now

58. In the next life

As opposed to say that it cannot happen

Suppose that we say that it is possible

For continuity to occur without a starting point…

59. Before the beginning

You must understand
That before coming here
You had never felt fear

       This is not your truth

60. The butterflies of love

When you finally meet your soul mate,

The true reflection of your self, your eternal counterpart

There are no butterflies fluttering in your stomach

For it is not your body that feels then, not anymore, but your essence

It is your silence that remembers

That part of you that is not physical, that which you perhaps never knew existed

That part of you in which cocoon magic, pure elation and absurd psychic connections

That part of you from which you salvage a sense of familiarity, a sort of precognitive foreshadowing infused with confusion

It is that part of you that screams that you have met before

That you know this person

From another place, another time, another life…a thousand wars

It is that part of you that mourns

Because you were not their first

Because you begin to doubt that you had ever loved anyone prior

Because you will now love beyond reason

Because the symphony of your heart has changed

Because that person will be your last

Like the ash of your final fire

Naturally

61. I will not let go

August, Puppeteer

You are the most beautiful scar on my body

I am entertained

62. Through the eyes of the blind

In your eyes, kind constant

I saw the infinite ways in which the soul could break

A caged mind at peace, plundering madness

That lies between the shadow and the self

In your flesh, kind constant

I found epics and limericks that burned my core...

The echo of life

A gentle shiver of freedom and abandon

And I ached to write you

The many intricacies of you

Your insubstantial grace

The quiet that you never unearthed

A universe of collapsed museums

And cursed crosses and sanctuaries

That dance on your dawn

Your restless darkness and eternal storms

The uncorrupted lines of your form

The bareness of your imprisonment

You

Only you

All of you

You, humbly

I ached to write nothing

But you

In Fibonacci

63. The spirit molecule

Close your eyes
Listen to silence absolute
Forget what you know
Go as far as you can go

Explode

64. The wheel

If I could prove to you that consciousness was not an accidental by-product of brain activity, would you still want to play with me?

65. The things that you forgot

It is not punishment

It is not reward anyhow

66. I was born like this

I am

A dance

A method

Naked

A word

That seeks caress and chemicals

In a prudently planned war

In which people no longer speak

Where death is inexpensive

I am

A dance

A rule

Naked

A touch

That of a virtuous scarlet

In a playfully concealed madhouse

One in which all are welcome

One in which life, untimely, is always fitting

I am

A dance

Not a happy dance

A screaming ecchymosis

Naked

A world

Pulled over my eyes

To keep me from the truth

Of my non-existence

67. When I go back home

If I should die tonight
May it be in your arms, old friend

      You make me feel alive

68. Everything, nothing

I am fragment and whole

       Perfect my story

69. Finality

I was with you all along

Printed in the United States
By Bookmasters